CW00550905

The Momentary Clock
Seventy-six poems

The momentary clock ticks without lenience,

with its small packets of ingratiating time.

These stitched moments ascend to form a life

from the sun-cast shadows at our wandering feet.

Other titles by Peter Hague

' Hope in the Heart of Hatred'
Twenty-nine poems

' Gain of Function'
One hundred and two poems

' Summer With The Gods'
Seventy-three poems

' Louder Prayers'
Seventy-one poems.

The Momentary Clock

THE MOMENTARY CLOCK

Seventy-six poems

Writing No.13

PETER HAGUE

The Momentary Clock

First Published in Autumn 2022
by Peter Hague Concept Design Art Direction

ISBN 978-1-8382746-9-6

Cover Design, layout, typography and cover art:
Peter Hague Concept Design Art Direction.

Also available in paperback: ISBN 978-1-8382746-8-9

A catalogue record for this book
is available from the British Library.

To the memory of my Brother.
Who died too young in 1994

"And there will be no point in leaving this stage of earth
with a full bag of energies digging at its grit:
I want to be distraught; I want to be wrung out;
I want to be the burned out shell of human existence
and human doubt. I want to go with the knowledge
that the last train has left the station
and is out there singing in the beautiful distance."

From 'A Firing Squad'

Contents

I. The Truth of Looking

II. The Savagery of Time

III. Zeus Inside My Clock

Contents continued

IV. The Silent Hill

V. Unfinished Thinking

Notes

In the years since Leonard Cohen's death in November 2016, I have written a small number of poems celebrating his own work and its influence on the world and in particular, on my own formative writings as a follower of his output since the late 1960s. Some of these poems have been published in my recent books and elsewhere, and in these latest pages you will find some more of those poems, which for me, seem a part of filling the space where he had been in my artistic life. I have always seen Cohen as something of a distant role model, almost a benefactor of the soul; a guiding force that enhanced many aspects of my life, certainly as regards his work ethic. The poems that remember him here are: 'Stranger Still in Utility Sunlight', 'I Did Not Want It Darker' and 'This Is Silence'. All these were first published in 'Fevers of the Mind' poetry.

The great American poet Theodore Roethke is also remembered here in the poems: 'Notes On Gardening' and 'The Way to Roethke'. There are also two poems first published in 'Hard Rain Poetry' by Fevers of the Mind in June 2022. They are: 'The Libertarian' and 'Where I Thought I Was'. A very personal poem called: 'A Day on Claypit Lane' was not resolved in time to appear in 'Hard Rain Poetry' and so resides here instead.

Four of the poems were first published on Twitter.

Momentary Clocks
Introduction becomes an essay

What started out as a brief introduction to that which might constitute a 'momentary clock', soon expanded into a longer examination, and seemed a relevant course of exploration at the beginning of this book of 'time-shaped' poems – that is to say, those experiences perhaps viewed through the macro-lens of the eye and the heart. I hope the reader will regard this introduction-come-essay, not as the ramblings of a man who has not yet found what he is looking for, but the workings of a man who is still looking – and who may sometimes faithfully presume his quest to be on the behalf of others. See this discourse as a bonus perhaps, containing as it does, some thoughts and concepts I have entertained from time to time, and also in my contemplations about life itself and the role poetry might play in it – even when poetry seemed lacking in acceptance or was mentally resisted by the orchestrated cacophony of daily concerns.

1 Each Shadow a Poem

The mood of this book is a broad observation of the subtle packets of time that shape and surround our lives, often bleeding into the lives of others. It is comprised of a variety of individual poems that represent their place in the adventure of the everyday world we find ourselves living in. The actual sense of time we are describing here is to be regarded as that portion of it which is measured in moments rather than seconds or smaller increments. Imagine the shadow of a sundial crossing a section of its face – a slow, sweeping, physical thing, inhabiting only a brief moment as it moves on – not drifting, but not favouring precision either – a mystery unveiling the mysteries. This is the momentary time we are considering now – the relentless moment – the broader sense of a moment. It is open to suggestion and possibility, and not quite as discourteous as the tedious work of an analogue clock or the sleight of hand of digital displays. And certainly not in the static chime of photographs, which so far as time is concerned are often sealed at both ends – a single 'frame' – not even a statement – an encapsulation that cannot be presumed to relate a full story; there is no mind to them – only unreliable memory or speculation. I will come back to the possibility of photographs in their doubtful role of *time machines* momentarily, meanwhile, even a seemingly static shadow is to be considered a clock and each shadow a poem, shaped by its own moment and awarded its own subtle velocity.

The time-shaped poem is always complete, we need only concern ourselves with the translation of it, which may require further contemplation, or a measure of humility. The sundial is an enchantment in itself; a living thing – humble in its various forms, each second becoming a momentary projection of potential knowing; a truth scribed by the Sun in a moving shadow that will never quite be drawn again. I hope the reader will come to understand these moments as a force, something similar to a symbiotic coalescence. One that helps to form the sudden reality of a time-shaped poem – but not just a demonstration of physics – there has to be *a mind to it*. With a sundial or some similar moving shadow, we can actually watch time in its worldly creation – an act falling into a settled presumption, or a parallel meditation – but there is no 'frame rate' as in the art of cinematography, the 'frames' are infinite – so who then will say that *time*, as a genuine preposition guiding our souls, is merely an invention of humankind based on a few not yet fully understood notions of physics and how we have instinctively come to record them?

Consequently, so far as intention goes, nothing has changed in the general presentation of all our existences and all that went before us – but the method of recording the passage of time in various media is our invention alone. This dates back to the earliest cave drawings that have remained intact, if ironically so, since the time of sun and erosion were not permitted to delete them, so these drawings were allowed to represent the sun itself – casting light across the face of the cavern – becoming the earliest form of clock. The momentary time spent drawing them into a presence remains intact inside their presence thereafter. They could call this first presence 'now' and its cycle, 'within the now', simply because there was nothing scribed before it. And later came the further acknowledgement of the Moon and stars and the hieroglyphs and the scriptures and paintings of the Old Masters, and so on – these are all momentary clocks in their way, both currently and in retrospect and have a future. Time spent on their production can be imagined and reproduced in a detail that does not require the perfect setting of exact imitation or required order – it can be both actioned and infinite, just by looking, and can therefore be said to be in some ways redeemable – or shared with the artist. This is not to trouble T. S. Eliot's consideration that if *all time is eternally present then all time is unredeemable.* It is not the same equation or understanding of time – certainly when given Eliot's presumed constraints of all time being present at once. The lazy sundial is necessarily wavering and imprecise, and thus time is presented or alludes us in different ways.

As a side issue, I have always thought it would seem plausible to add the limiting factor to Eliot's later work that regardless of his earlier studies into eastern religion and philosophy, he should have become somewhat restricted in his thoughts by his profound conversion in 1927 to Anglo-Catholic Christianity – a faith with particularly strict notions of precise liturgy, and whose narrative tends towards the traditional journey from creation to death and rebirth, as affirmed by the sacrifice of Jesus – Son of God and man. Thus – *in my beginning is my end.**

Although Eliot's collected masterpiece 'Four Quartets' remains a meditation filled with references to eastern enlightenment, it is overtly Christian in its resolution. It was also written in the shadow of World War Two, in the outward looking spirit of loyalty and hope and given Eliot's rightful status as a truly acclaimed 'great poet', it can sometimes seem almost the word of God, though perhaps with an independent magnificence. And that is what I mean when I say: it is not the same equation or understanding of time – the lazy sundial remains half mysterious and somewhat infinite, like spreading a hand of playing cards.

2 Imagination and the Thrust of Willpower

In my own thinking, I have purposefully kept myself on the outskirts of religious belief, so that my reasoning may make judgments that are at least not coloured by the foundations of liturgy. It is not to say though that I have discarded the possibility that the universe may be controlled by a great power – what we might call, in our blind state, either supernatural or practical – the workings of which, may be embedded in the mystery of so-called 'dark energy', or in the discreet packets of subatomic particles – things we name, but still know little or nothing about.

In the sense of continuation and fractured history, the

* *from: T. S. Eliot's: Four Quartets*

turning regime of readjusting civilisations and the repetitive experience of overlapping layers of developing society, can lead us to see what is possible in the future – if only by imagination and the thrust of willpower. Humankind is very good at harvesting its legislation from the imagined future – it dreams up its bag of notable possibilities and moulds a reality. Many of the essentials we have today were mere thoughts a few decades ago – or mere movies ago, where cinematic ideas ferment into facts. Our world has changed its viewpoint continually, and embedded in its presentation of things, from cave-drawings to cellphones, there is a constant drive to communicate and tell ourselves something we did not know before, or perhaps needed confirmation of.

It is also true, that given hindsight and the possession of such tools for change, we can often see the possibilities for the future in our past – especially if we consider the clues offered in the triumphs and subtleties embedded in the broader picture – and I mean by that: on the world scale, such as the pyramids of Giza. Their staggering accuracy of placement and geometry is said to be barely achievable today, even with our current precision technology. A single detail at least worthy of contemplation is to look at a map of all the landmasses on Earth and notice that these three related pyramids of Giza are positioned at the approximate centre of it all – a practical endorsement of wonder beyond expected scale. These three pyramids, which were once faced with a smooth limestone casing that made them shine like stars in the sunlight, seem also visually linked to the three stars that make up the 'belt' in the constellation of Orion; particularly by the offset position of the smallest pyramid and also by the angle of one of the four long shafts in the Great Pyramid itself. Before the axis of planet Earth was moved along its twenty-six-thousand-year cycle by the process of precession, this shaft pointed exactly at the stars in Orion's Belt and will eventually return to that position. So this view from the past may also stand as evidence of the future – in full regard of the idea of circular time.

Some observers denounce the current presentation of these pyramids as nothing but a ragged pile of stones, but that is the point they are missing, because all this detail between one abstraction and the next is the continuing emergence of new targets for entropy to work on and rock the motion, rather like the living crib – an eternal chaos of rebirth – an engine of true deliverance – because beneath this seemingly endless flux and the bones of infinity, and at the heart of these so-called "piles of rubble" sits the perfect mathematics that scaled them all those thousands of years ago. Not forgetting that every object and the sum of all their parts are all moving at a different velocity to each other, regardless of how infinitesimal that measurement might be. Considering that the pyramids may have been constructed well before the currently estimated date of four and a half thousand years ago they are a solid testament to the geometric knowledge they are based on, which also seems to predate the classical historical models, such as *Pi* and the *metre*. If this is true, then that fact alone will show our beginning is certainly in our end – and yet time will also be in some way redeemable. Some future presence may well see the circle squared in its fullest sense.

The Great Pyramid, for what ever purpose, seems to speak its words to us in pure mathematics. Perhaps because language cannot be relied upon through the coming ages? Think of the pyramids as the ultimate sundial – the ultimate momentary clock. In the future, if words are redundant, will we speak numerically? Will poetry be lines of equations that somehow tune our minds to provoke feeling and understanding? Music seems close to that already.

In an abstract sense, a picture on a wall with the light of the Sun crossing it is a momentary clock, scanned in a new time, which is called now – just like a sundial or the light-rays passing across the words of a time-stamped newspaper. If you have seen a butterfly reposition its wings in sunlight, or you have watched a ladybird exploring your finger – all this is the momentary clock, accomplished by a new transfiguration – everything is the 'clock'. A coffee spoon can be part of the process, or an afternoon, stretched across a floor beside us, as registered by Eliot in 'The Love Song of J. Alfred Prufrock'; or by 'Death in the Afternoon' cheered on by Hemingway; or "...a car slides by on grease," observed by Robert Lowell. They all have their shadows, moving over the face of their dial, as light moved over the face of the deep at the time of creation, as suggested by Christianity. And it need not matter that the faith is upheld in this thought, it is enough to know that humankind's borrowed words are across the face of this appropriated idea – our own deep. The complication of moments has become our own timepiece with something worthy manipulating the light and shade.

3 A Tale of Caution

Time is a soup, stirred by physics and we are part of it; though we have to learn to live within it and find our place. The soup is a method of constant presentation and we, as individuals, are able to observe it; to explore it and by our own actions, attempt to change it. If God has handed some part of his stewardship to us, we must rise to that challenge without arguments of oppressive detail and the primitive strictures of fundamentalism or invented guilt. Beginnings are never too far from the journey and are present at the end in the form of reason – as though reason is a requirement of progression or rebirth: *"In the beginning was the Word, and the Word was with God, and the Word was God"*. This is a momentary statement of the conditions of omnipotent adjudication, regardless of what the adjudicator might be – an eternal moment on the sundial perhaps. In this case it is where Christianity begins and returns its reason – the journey being a play of demonstrative scenes, which from a secular viewpoint are merely broad moments of seemingly unconnected physics – the actual *Soup*.

In a 'particular scene', as we may call it, say in Dealey Plaza in Dallas on 22 November 1963 at the local time of 12.30pm, every part was its own poem and its own reason – every brick or breath, every blade of grass – every particle of dust and sunlit smoke was its own momentary clock in all its minute particulars. I mention this, in the context of an extreme example in order to verify the breadth and scale of what is meant when I use the innocent phrases: 'momentary clock' or 'time-shaped' poems – which in themselves carry no rigidity of form and could be something as random as a single emotion, unmet by the presence of corroboration. There is no finality or greater cause here for the basis of a poem that may be more worthy than another; not even those concerning the death of a president. The poems available at this point, in all its various arrangements in time, are infinite, and if anything was likely to make these moments unredeemable it would be that – the sheer size of the data. Yet given that realisation, there is still no final truth about any of it – things can still be investigated and changed – and there is just so much information then – a momentary clock – certainly redeemable, since the truth is neither accepted or sought to any great value. Neither is it sought in the nature of things as opposed to human politics. To understand this, it is best to imagine a world where the human dilemma has no priority over dust.

I chose this particular example, not only because of the starkness of truth and natural indifference envisaged at once, but also because it can be used to demonstrate the possibility of distorted truth in legitimate reasoning – or give a false reading of it. Also to cover the possibility of flaws in human observation, which carry the natural hazards and serendipity of mistranslation.

The 'factor' I am about to mention came totally from left field and is well beyond the normal scale of eyes playing tricks. It was a mystery which came to be known as 'Umbrella Man': the name given to a spectator standing in the crowd. He was only a few feet from the position where President John F. Kennedy received the first bullet wound, leading to his complete assassination a few car-lengths further on. Although it was not raining, the man in question had raised an open, black umbrella and was spinning it in a clockwise direction as though giving the signal to fire. For years after, no one knew the identity of this man or what was meant by his suspicious behaviour – not until he finally came forward to exonerate himself – albeit fifteen years later. His name was Louie Steven Witt and it turns out he was making a silent demonstration aimed at Kennedy's father, who had been US Ambassador in 1939 and had backed the then British Prime Minister, Neville Chamberlain in his appeasement of Hitler and the Nazi party. It appears that Witt had nothing to do with the assassination at all; his being there at the time and 'signalling' with his umbrella was just a coincidence that looked very suspicious for a very long time. He said using an umbrella as a protest was a throw back, relating to Chamberlain's signature habit of always carrying an umbrella with him. Umbrella Man can be partly seen behind a road sign on the Zapruder film and on various photographs taken that day. What other incidents of accidental misdirection are embedded into the countless momentary clocks sewn deep into those infamous seconds?

4 Lies to Credulous Hearts

Because I have already alluded to photography as a possible merchant of time there is a new word to consider. I use it in the phrase: "trite adventures in photomentology"* and which I perceive as the recent trend of over-saturating and over-sharpening the beauty of nature and other phenomena. Not in the true application of artistic

* *from the poem: 'A Lack of Effort in Wider Thought'*

photography, where adventure is of course allowed, but in the strict medium of it – as though this tampering reveals a position closer to the truth in a given day to day scene than actually exists, other than in the manipulation of the technician or the marketed dream. These 'parody' photographs should not be pretending to be any more than technical prowess; or perhaps just 'fun with film'.

Similar techniques are also found in the genuine war photography predominately influencing the protests of the 1960s, although this was almost always presented in monochrome, which is a prerequisite with full immunity where death and honour are concerned, and with the true grain of the fast film showing in the print as an inevitable feature of the process. The definition of 'photomentology' is more in the mind than in the photograph. It has no such pedigree beyond its digital tamperings, which are all contrived to enhance some already beautiful photographs.

Although this endless capacity for modification is unquestionably indispensable when producing art, it is not so welcome when slaughtering the beauty of nature by bearing false-witness to it. Only the universe has the infinite palette and only physics can render the true livery of its word.

This trick of presentation can be thought of as "the enhanced discolouration of the human truth" and perhaps has some merit or reason when considering early colour

Polaroid prints, though once again, Polaroid images were instant and 'on-site' and very much part of a strictly observed development process – the photographer was only permitted to choose this sunnier style of photography for its look – as an option – and with all limitations accepted. Over-saturated colours were creations of the film media beyond anything pure nature or pure photography had to offer for any particular scene. A beautiful sense of this was captured by Paul Simon in his song: 'Kodachrome', named after another old film stock that: *"Gives those nice bright colors/gives us the greens of summers/makes you think all the world's a sunny day..."* *. The processing of this film was also heavily restricted – each roll was in reality, three emulsion layers, each sensitised to the primary colours. Their relationship to each other only being fully realised later in time, well after the photography session and in the factory processing itself – which incidentally, was also legally restricted for many years as a matter of copyright.

I should now offer the co-incidental, and perhaps ironic detail, that it was the Super 8 movie version of Kodachrome that was loaded into Zapruder's camera on the day of Kennedy's assassination, but as we have seen, the momentary clock refuses to render itself to over-sharpened and over-saturated possibilities – as though this irrefutable fact reveals a position closer to the truth than is ever present. The scene in Dallas is flooded with truth, but never

* *from: 'Kodachrome' by Paul Simon*

over-burdened, or even satisfied by it. Josiah Thompson, the author who coined the name Umbrella Man, also observed it was a "beautiful day in the neighbourhood".

The Zapruder film has now taken on an iconic status, partly as a way of translating it, since its production has nothing to do with truth – as we have seen, it is overwhelmed by its own testimony and is a good example of what is missing from the as yet unfathomable loyalty of the momentary clock. Tragic as it is, the film, with its dark margins and the secret depths of its sprocket holes, has welcomed a study far beyond forensic science and has become a work of art – elevated to a state of pilgrimage and spiritual meditation.

In some senses, there may be a contradiction here because I think these sunny options for film and photographs, minus their factory deviation, were also akin to the passing of the sun across the face of a sundial. Who knows what moon and stars may have guided them in the dark cavern of pre-development – especially when I look at them now, with a time consideration – because what you perceive when viewing this moving finger is very much an antiquated sensation that we have no control over. It is an ever-moving shroud – always on its way to its predetermined truth; not caring to improve the quality of its colours – or find their true precision; it is always what it was, even before it left the factory and met the full circle of the 'sunny day'. Only the subject matter is a variable, though many conform to the myriad innovations of family moments. And there is no limit to the 'frame rate' on the face of a momentary sundial – neither up nor down – so all motion can be captured in a perfect stillness and perfect stillness captured in motion. Yet what defines 'stillness' or 'now' when the whole illusion that surrounds our being is loaned to us by the precarious delivery of time through the constant measure of light-speed – thus forcing the universe adrift with its milliseconds of delay? It would seem prudent now, to point out that the distance to our eyes from the moving shadow are also both independent and variable and thus are each subject to tiny variations of time and space. In short, we are something else.

Time is its own truth under the guidance of light; and its own eventual judgement that has nothing to do with us. And the key to the future of humanity is surely best conducted through humility alone. And after all the bitter words and bribed influence, humankind still has the capacity to redeem itself – but only in its own dream – that propitious realm of disengaged time that does not care about the trivialities of civilisational propaganda – and where we *dream up our bag of notable possibilities and mould our true reality.*

It is a new realm of welcome mystery,
beyond which, we may see its silence wink at us,
like the birds in the air or the face in the crowd,
which is our own face
and has a blank expression.
It is a look of knowing –
it is the untapped enigma –
or the solitude that abounds
when the last train is going.
When the station is empty
and there is nothing to lie about;
when all propaganda
is renounced on all sides.
There will still be voices,
claiming the truth of their doctrine;
we will teach them the influence
of unblemished forgiveness.
Let it come from the soul of a heartfelt humility,
that will end the slow folly
of presumed human righteousness –
that glorification of uncertified trust –
that deadly counterbalance
to the true issues of misery.

Peter Hague

The Momentary Clock

THE MOMENTARY CLOCK

Seventy-six poems

Presented in five parts:

I. *The Truth of Looking*
II. *The Savagery of Time*
III. *Zeus Inside My Clock*
IV. *The Silent Hill*
V. *Unfinished Thinking*

Writing No. 13

PETER HAGUE

The palace of Versailles is too vast to look at,
and is stiffened by statues of gold and blackened bronze.
They languish in fountains to cool their history,
as slippers of water splash past their mouths.
They remember when silence was an imagined ruminant –
when nothing worth saying was ever said;
certainly not in this kingdom of kings –
or in the wheeze of the dead.
Versailles is too grand to think itself necessary –
it forgets its name, like a borrowed sun.
And at least once in every hundred years
it stains an old sire's royal blue breath.
It is trodden through by tourists then,
who constantly forget why they came this way,

I. The Truth of Looking

as the sun moves with them, room by room,
and they examine themselves in the hall of vanity;
they register their presence in redundant frames –
non-entities in the honesty of token mirrors.
Later, in the modern cliché of a hotel room,
a single mirror is a depressing spectre.
A thousand eyes stare out of an awkward history,
spend measuring the harvest of a hardening skin.
Each eye burnt-out by the shock of godly.
The palace of Versailles is too vast to look at,
and is stiffened by statues of gold and blackened bronze.
They languish in fountains to cool their history,
as slippers of water splash past their mouths.
They remember when silence was an imagined ruminant
when nothing worth saying was ever said;
certainly not in this kingdom of kings –
or in the wheeze of the dead.
Versailles is too grand to think itself necessary –

A Secret Youth

I rise to see the garden rebelling.
I see it through the frame of an open sash window.
Arranged is a French girl, working with flowers,
her hair tied back in trailing tails.
She pours the future from a fountain spout –
the lingering mercy of a watering can –
she paints the better beauty of its rainbowed life
onto pleading roots, one by one.

These plants are limp – a beseeching youth;
they beg for the showering miracle of the rose.
And might, in distillations of sundialed shadows,
allow these moments of summer to flow on.
It is a scene uninterrupted by sliding time,
whereas I, in my hunched age of broken bones,
have bled all the water from my paper skin.
I have become Death of Moth – Husk of Rose.

I went skittering then, in search of youth –
an imperfect creature – sick of itself –
labouring the dashed hopes of tattered wings
that I could not steer to alight on anything.
It was a twisted braid of scented air,
then called my journey to the other side –
to gather the iridescence of mother of pearl
and shine as a butterfly – an abstraction – a slide.

Notes On Gardening

To the memory of Theodore Roethke. 1908-1963

The rain swept under bushes of fire
that spat out their hatred in clouds of steam.
And with a hissing sound to suffer in,
like hell's inferno might think to make –
a carcass whistle;
a potato in a bonfire;
a candle, burning down its wicked threat
to the icing of a birthday cake.

My bones ache.
They crack with the injustice of an unforgiving spade,
and I am forced to find other ways to scour my dirt –
ways to skirt around a seasonal pain, in this,
the hardest ever stoney ground.
Down in the dirt ways,
where the roots will not betray their stem
and cling to rocks, like children to a mother's hem.
Or I may return to the scourge of a rake
and re-deal the rogue seeds of relentless reclamation –
and also the broken bones of scattered men –
a cluster bomb for the following year.
If I am still here, I will pretend not to notice them.

I will plant my impatient fingers in patient pots
and water them with acid, regardless of pain.

I will watch them grow, long and skeletal,
like my ancient hair in the wire of rain.

And under my next birthday's candlelight,
these curious fingers will grow into a humid air.
They will smash through the sweat of greenhouse panes
and feel their way back to the welcoming house –
back to the piano they have always loved
but were finger-blind – too fat of flesh to play.
The piano is a thing with a voice made of wood;
something that grew in some far-off forest.
A thing with herculean chords, somehow to endure,
that my fingers are long enough to finally take on –
profound enough, with their boney lips, to say:
"We can span the whole of suburbia now
for an F minor 6th or a B major 7th,
without that impromptu, erroneous A."

And now, having cultivated the gift
of advanced musical form
and forced its staves into my human frame,
I will be able to declare with appropriate zest
that this is agony – this is Eden.
This is gardening
at its best.

The Truth of Looking

The palace of Versailles is too vast to look at
and is stiffened by statues of gold and blackened bronze.
They languish in fountains to cool their history,
as slippers of water splash past their mouths.
They remember when silence was delivered as a ruminant;
when nothing worth saying was ever said.
Certainly not in this kingdom of kings
or in the wheeze of the dead.

Versailles is too grand to think itself necessary –
it forgets its name, like a borrowed sin.
And at least once in every hundred scandals
it stains an old sire's royal blue breath.
It is trodden through by tourists, time and again,
who constantly forget why they came this way –
as the sun moves with them, room by room,
and they examine themselves in the hall of vanity.
They register their presence in redundant frames –
non-entities in the honesty of token mirrors.

And later, in the modern cliché of hotel rooms
a single mirror is a depressing source.
A thousand eyes stare from an awkward history,
spent measuring the harvest of passing skin.
Each eye made blind by the shocks of godly men –
and the exquisite gold of a traversing sun.

The Luxury of Private Emotions

If you are happy, make a moment of your minutes –
reward yourself a veiled smile.
You can frown again later, into the public arena,
where the iron cross is nailed to the struggle of each mile –
where they pour their mockery of unrelenting bile
onto the modest fabric of your beautiful quest.
You can always fool them with a grieving eye
and the taut anxiety of omitted trust.

Clockwork Poems

You can wind my key and make me speak;
make me reveal what I meant at the time.
For I am a clockwork poem – poised for the telling –
a creature in resonance with the envy of weapons.
I am armoured with precision and subtle pledges;
angled with a soft heart, made good with bone.
I sleep one-eyed, behind the shards of palings –
and the billboard clouds of enormous fences.

I will return to my position via the autotomy of time;
discarding whole decades in an easy process.
The key that winds – unlocks the door
and the truth of the poem steps out of its frame.
You will shoulder me proudly – as a trusted stranger,
stumbling with the duty of accepted pursuance;
matching my steps through the space between ages
and settling for adventure in place of doubt.

I will guide you beyond the scope of your peers;
past all experiments and beneath all pretensions.
I will take you to the truth I found in mansions,
and in all the crevices of the passing years.
Your eyes have the energy of the coiling spring –
your mind is the key that turns again.
Turn it to trigger these clockwork poems
and prepare for the dichotomy of a cog's embrace.

linear IgA
Refers to a rare skin disease.

I hate the phrase 'white knuckle ride' –
it sounds like fashion, yet I wear scars.
None may notice my blistering fingers –
oozing yellow behind cotton gloves.
Or their festering nails – sheathed in night –
beneath a mothering fabric of hopeful balm.

They turn savage in an ointment
of poisoning blight.
Yet seem to calm.

I hate the phrase – 'white knuckle ride'.
I still ride the fear though – as deep as any other –
and cling on to the world in much the same way
in the absence of deliverance
or a living mother.

Arrogance Finds New Make-up

And dark energy
is the darkness
of human souls –
inflicting on the stars
what they could not do
while alive
on a brittle Earth –
under close examination.

First published on Twitter – 11 March 2022

The Libertarian

I spent some time with hatred
but will loath no more.
My desire is to free my liberty
from its own locked door.
I locked it in my youth –
rent with misery – and at war.

First published in 'Hard Rain Poetry'– Fevers of the Mind June 2022

The Results of Hate Crime Law
The confiscation of freedom of speech

Frustrated people are tumid and dangerous –
you feel their anger on uncomfortable pavements.
You cross the street but cannot avoid them;
they own the dark-side of every ravine.
They hide behind windscreens and look to be angry,
silenced by the laws of criminalised hatred.
It has removed their option of a mere bad mood –
an important factor of their way of life.
Frustrated people have a need to vent;
it is treated like a buffer to absorb pure violence.
Anger can exist in inappropriate words
or in the crude reliance of age-old intentions.
The noble savage art of disagreeable conversation
is an honest charade that sets people talking –
voicing their freedom to state legitimate thoughts
that might eventually cool into a settlement of peace.

Laws Against Liberty

Taut between them, the centrist battlers,
have frayed the authority of our moderate nation.
Binding our song of treasured eccentricity
into a fearful storm of doubtful correctness.
This tormenting breath of vitriolic words
has scribed the new laws of our lost liberties –
gouging them in silence – a replacement for concrete –
a new stringent bedrock of constitutional graffiti.

But no one can read graffiti these days
when it shouts in the whispers of a bullshit style –
when endorsed by councillors of dubious intent,
in their hateful revenge of ironic bile.
They think the streets are no longer for commerce –
a fever of manipulation for the experimentally diverse.
Not truly caring about the threat of imbalance,
nor the instability of a stolen sense of place.

Nor can they hear what else may speak,
neath its random cacophony of tidings and errors.
They have replaced your opinions
and your freedom of speech
with the protectionist fear of judicial retribution.
Everyone else
and all the monsters
go free.

Saying Goodbye

The pen I put to paper
left a letter in your eye.
It might have been an oh,
or maybe just a why?

Comfort Poem at Sea
To the memory of Hart Crane. 1899-1932

It cannot be death without a poem –
something to wrap my agony inside before I sleep;
before I rest beneath this vertical tide
that falls away, so steep.

Write the words across my sheets –
the billowing pages of unfurled letters
are the only wrappings I can take;
the only sails that will carry me forth,
beyond the chains of a snagging wake.

Can you not just see I want to sleep?
Let the weight of words
carry me down
and deep.

The American poet, Hart Crane, jumped off the stern of a steamship in 1932.

Head Shot
Poem from the Grassy Knoll

Swimming in your pool – the blue of your bluest car,
you are blessed with riches and poor health.
Your hair though – your hair is always in pieces –
always portraying something else;
a barnacle loaf, made of organised tufts,
clinging to a sensible, presidential style.
A shape that women like, nonetheless,
and mobile young men have strived to attain.
Your teeth are the whitest purity of white –
a beacon in that forest of family and fortunes;
a registered compensation of an influential ménage;
a centring for the whole soul of humanity's hopes.
It is a journal of glory – seen through confident eyes –
all awash with the stars of a charismatic smile.

And a well-hidden brain –
what secrets that complex domain could claim?
Resting between the dark ambition
of politics and thighs.

You hold the patent for American looks
and America looks somewhat like you:
slightly exaggerated; a version of Victoriana;
lost in the new world and not quite true.
Yet still somehow royal and desirable –

mimicking the ornate, with a floral confidence.

You are haunted by death though –
and grossly too...
before they die, rich boys have to find
something better to do.
And death, before it finally arrives,
is a provocateur of urgent days –
it underscores the expectant desperations
of why we are – and who?

You need something to take your mind off that hair;
hair that now worries me, being an unofficial assassin.
There is always a longing to share one's moment –
even when spiralling into permanent chaos.
You tried wind and sailboats to shape your current,
but nothing reliable – nothing you could steer –
the statesman in the mirror, chained to limousine-leather,
not seeing the playboy with unruly hair.

A bullet though... one that truly seemed to care –
might part your life a different way –
along with some lawless, unexplained magical stray?
some day...

The People in the Background

There they are, dancing in the back of 1966.
Or walking down the high street a year ago.
I wonder who they are and if they still exist?
Walking on the wake of our under-tow.

They will survive us for sure.
They will survive us forever.
They will even be able to remain with their friends.
Dancing live to still popular music –
they will linger in youth and always together.

We were never filmed and stitched into backgrounds;
we lived our lives where the sea cancels the shore.
Finally sliding off the face of the calendar,
not even close to a cutting-room floor.

The Momentary Clock

The momentary clock has no true hands
and keeps us guessing – one fragment to the next.
Each moment is an act, or a poem, or a joy.
Every memory, half-forgotten – is a girl? – is a boy?
Every creak on the stair becomes the closing of a door.
Or we are sitting in a chair
and there is peace – then war.
And every triumph has a bloodied shore,
where bodies wash up like bones in soup
and we are alive with miracles
or we are lost in a loop.

It is two o'clock in the afternoon
and I am late for a meeting
that will not matter soon.
Things become too late to bother the mind,
freeing time to spare for details and such –
and looking restless – but back in touch.
I am stuck in traffic; I am in mid-air.
I am riding an avalanche called Cohen's despair.
I fall from the bus and I am crying in a downpour –
but cannot hear the sound of my hysterical laughter.
I turn away from the taxi driver's windscreen stare –
I turn toward the taunting of his sun-blistered pity.

The car has become a boat, ready for the sinking –

The Momentary Clock – continued...

where the pavement is a safe and timely shore.
It walks together with our brazen terrace,
with black, iron railings and a silhouetted glow –
or the big city block of stainless steel
leans back from a blizzard of sudden snow.
I am dripping on an escalator, or dry in a lift,
with my briefcase frozen or my shopping bag lost;
with my carefully wrapped impervious gift;
or the cruel demise of my damp cigarette.

My boots slap across the marble floor.
My high-heels avoid the traps of grill or grate.
And after minutes of discussion and hours of listening,
I am still unavoidably late.
I am in a cinema – I am in a bar.
I am travelling home – I am through the door.
I am sitting with my thoughts in a devouring chair.
I am alone in my bed – I am over there.
I am borrowed from tomorrow; I am just setting up.
I am a hand or a claw – a wing or a foot.
I am the shadow on the face of the momentary clock.
I am the key in the slot to wind it shut.
I am losing my skin to creases and lines.
I am guided through life by momentary signs.
I am dead on a bed, or worse – I am born.
I am smooth and invisible –

we attack at dawn.

The time on the face of the clock
had slipped down
like a Salvador Dali:
3.15
bent of mind.

I cleansed myself
of my favourite mistakes,
and languished in a new
unreal reality,
with distorted chimes.
There will be a brave new world soon,
with warped clocks and violence,
and the people surviving

2

II. The Savagery of Time

will need to be straight –
though bent of mind.
The time on the face of the clock
had slipped down
like a Salvador Dali:
3.15
bent of mind.
I cleansed myself
of my favourite mistakes,
and languished in a new
unreal reality,
with distorted chimes.
There will be a brave new world soon,
with warped clocks and violence,
and the people surviving
The time on the face of the clock
had slipped down
like a Salvador Dali:

The Poor Pariah

Where will the world go now without Russia –
without its complex weave of power and monstrosity?
Where will the world move to sit apart
from these endless instalments of misread glory;
from beyond this confusion of the rebirth of empire.

The philosophical conversation of war and peace
still burns in the anxiety of the Russian hearth –
with the crime and punishment of jealous blood,
where the vanity of conquerers justifies death.

We will need a place where their guns are silent,
now we have found our own guns wanting or misplaced.
We will disguise our weakness with sanctions and aid,
while firing sterile criticism at logistical targets –
wounding ourselves with the backlash of expectation;
falling for the politics of jingoistic representation.

Mediocrity has been embraced by the crumbling West
and nursed to a position of fragile health.
We will conduct a proxy war of pompous psychology,
passing forth munitions from an imagined safety –
always underestimating the crude march of ambition
and the patriotic fervour in the idiot soul.

First published on Twitter – 10 March 2022

And Death Shall Have No Opinion?

If I wear your flag on my lapel
will it help you win the futility of war?
Or will you be displaced by reckless courage –
buried beneath the illusion you were fighting for.
My badge of promises may not be secure;
it may lead you up a deadly path –
where the earth is scorched and the trees grotesque
and we all play dead in the aftermath.

9th March 2022

'The Poor Pariah' and '…Death Shall Have No Opinion?', were a response to the Russian invasion of Ukraine.

For what it's worth, the two previous poems contain references to some of the great novels of Russian literature and also, in the above title, a reference to one of Dylan Thomas's great poems.

First published on Twitter – 18 March 2022

Our Depression is a Trance – Despair is a Vessel

The road to despair is the road to freedom.
Depression will take you part way there
but real freedom requires despair –
and will need some profound thinking.

A trance-like state will never do,
you will want a shovel to dig yourself deep,
and for later too –

Depression caught in mid-despair
is an anchor – it will nail you there;
symbolically fix you to an elaborate mast
under the telling weight of its dragging host.

To escape the pitiless – slewing tides,
you will need the ability to sail your ship;
you may sail on anything that slides.

Your despairing vessel is a bouquet of sails –
rig them sincerely until despair blows in.
There is still beauty in that unexplored sea,
and in the irrational doubt of noble whim.

Seek out the cargo of your new despair
and the inconsequential state of being there.

The Awakening Eye

On this, the bleakest of bleak days,
the sun still shines as warm as life,
and people draw smiles from the happy light.
And nothing cares; nothing moves;
nothing might.
Except the zipping paths of early wasps
that map the reference of an apple tree
in its full dimensions – all three.
There is also a monitoring of complacency here,
growing out of the warmed-up, earthly tensions.
They are sustained in the patterns of freedom and order,
embedded in the stone of this ruthless garden.
It is the structural failing of mild anxiety
that has fooled springtime out of its idle bed –
has cast it back to thinking-on;
listening to the song of a violent summer.

Everything is gauged
with an inherent sense
of dread.

All this patient facade of incremental joy
is not just the dark work of a cruel chaos.
It is the work of heroes, who will feel the surge
of a murderous existence beating forth.

We, This Poem

We, this poem, parade in broken lines.
We stand at attention – a ragged army.
We seek only to help you with your local vengeance –
you must not fall between untested plans.
I will speak harshly to the rank and file
and order each line to adore your leadership.
We will instil confidence at every turn –
you needn't fear a betrayal of your hollow self.
I will whisper the treasures of endless plunder,
paying close attention to the promise of gold.
Also to the savagery of taking scalps
and of running amok with fearful words.
There will be a special mission to settle old scores –
a popular enticement, yet a weaker ploy.
It is used by the leaders of mercenary souls,
whispering madness into darkening hearts.
It is also a ruse to subvert the rumours of doubt
that pervade mens' minds before the money is dealt.
And a bonus retribution for those stood too long
in the shadow of hierarchy and unworthy buffoons.

A Poem Takes Time...

A poem takes time...
I spend much of it trying not to rhyme.
Yet my brain gets caught in the teeth of a cog,
churning its pool of limiting words –
my head sucked into a wellington boot –
then stuck – head first – in the mind of a bog.

Where I Thought I Was

Take me to where I thought I was –
take me to where I've been.
Show me the shallow paradise
of somewhere in-between.

Nothing new may pass these eyes –
none of your polished – twisted lies.
I loved the past – now chastised –
when we were stylish and obscene.

First published in 'Hard Rain Poetry'– Fevers of the Mind June 2022

Ages Blessed and Fooled

Me to a mirror

At the age of sixty-one
you can reverse your years to sixteen
but it will make no difference –
you will still be a fool,
looking for ideas and distance;
lost in a new world that speaks itself
backwards.

At the age of sixty-two
you can reverse your years to twenty-six
but it will make no difference – at twenty-six
you led yourself down a garden path
and grew blue hydrangeas in acid blood.

When you are sixty-three
you can reverse your age to thirty six
but it will make no difference;
you made enough mistakes
in the preceding years
to void your future as a reliable companion.

When you are sixty-four
you can reverse your years to forty-six
but it will make no difference;
you will still have the guile

to ensure both paths are untaken –
and not look back from either one.

At sixty-five
you can reverse your years to fifty-six
but it will make no difference;
you are far enough from your beginnings now
to seek closer destinations than the promised land.
You will know for the first time
that sleep is not failure.

At the age of sixty-six
you can reverse your years to sixty-six
but it will make no difference.

At the age of sixty-seven
you can reverse your years to seventy-six
            and so on... making new numbers;
with the age of an infant and the mind of a child.
But it will make no difference
and seems compulsory.

I Will Not Gather Dust
A Birthday

My extinguishing breath blew sugared dust
beyond my companion tablecloth.
And I counted the many shards
now filling this room –
this primal doom –
this room as still as candle light.

They shone beyond my breath of words,
as letters in a page of moving sky –
or at least suggesting they might not die
for several minutes of contemplation.
For this was my existence; my book of days –
my cake – my yearly wage.
My scripted passage to another page,
written in the candles of a scorched salvation.

And after an acceptance of devolved power,
I cut out the frame of an unseen door.
It swung out a slice of this generic hour –
a momentary forging of death and joy.

The Isolation Of Walls And Universal Spaces

The world is a wall – it curves around its form –
creating the physics of a gravitational ball.
We stand on its crust, together and alone;
each axis separate – by the smallest of degrees –
the minute seconds that make our clocks
			unique.
Each head is protracted to a different point in space –
all wrapped in the elemental light-years
			of interwoven lace.
Our hands never touching,
by the method of sound or signs –
but connected by the astonishing ripples
of curved expanding lines.
These are the ripples of old-fashioned talk –

remnants of attempts to paint the randomness of sparks –

the whisperings in the chambers
between hollow human walls,
where we passed our eyes to reckless lips
and lit the dark with words.

The Savagery of Time

The time on the face of the clock of pain
had slipped down,
like a Salvador Dali –
3.15 and bent of mind.

I cleansed myself of my favourite mistakes
and languished in a lucid pool
of uncertain reality.
And with distorted chimes.

There will be a brave new world coming soon,
with warped clocks and violent hands.
And those surviving
will need to be straight of thought –
though bent of mind.

Post-mode(rn)ism(?)

Let us slip along these true lines here –
while stuck to them all with patient glue.
Award ourselves some abusive words
to challenge their scope of retribution.
Let us eulogise the foulest fevers,
and a musical score with brute notation –
all written-backwards by a silent mind,
yet one scarce of bread and logistical details.
Let us wash ourselves with stifling chords
that vibrate only beyond the stratosphere.
Let us become leaders and stand with crowds –
claiming true parity with our victory over sand.
Analyse the plight of the crown in darkness
and the darker Holy Land of dubious light.
There you have it – one-eyed king –
you are now the king of everything.
Let us cause the bedlam of meek exclusion
to erupt with blame and political satire.
Watch the collapse of the joke-filled arena,
and the ultimate orgasm of plentiful aporia.
They start by admitting this world is over
by merely suggesting some talk of a *coming*.
Or feel it deeper in the sense of *ressentiment* –
French and dripping with a fluid revenge;
they taste of hemlock and nameless stardust.
Yes the world is over. I am here to tell it.

The Art of Generalisation

I have no knowledge or learning.
I have studied many things;
I have looked and envied –
but do not listen to my comprehension
or my yearnings. I have learned nothing
except the art of generalisation.

The world is parading before your eyes,
yet also beyond your tools of understanding.
Think for yourself and trust the hour.
You will find the ideals you need to study –
they will promise assistance
to imagined goals.

Art and aesthetics will blind your soul,
with its bland dramatics of pretence and immersion.
Generalisation is a useful expansion;
it will enable the inclusion or omission of specifics.
You can narrow your thoughts then,
to a simple conclusion:

The values of ugliness, ignorance and disgrace
have an equal place in bliss and wonder.
Do not let the aesthetics of beauty
drag you under.

Blood Is Infuriating

They say blood is thicker than innocent water.
I hold with water.
Water is clear and hides nothing –
it sweats out its toil like a clarity from God.
It joins with sky, out in the offing –
evaporating in an absolution of pure clouds.

Blood is opaque and not to be trusted –
it is dilute with a jealousy that congeals in air.
It clots like bile and burns the muscles.
It constricts its arteries as we gasp for breath.
Blood leaches into soil, like a busy traitor,
wiping muddy footprints and becoming death.

Water can be stored as a cooling solid
and can sail its truth on a hopeful sea.
And when blood boils we can boil some water
for the universal comfort of ordinary tea.

The Death of My Brother
Written many years later.

It is time to say the final words.
They have been trapped for years
inside an unforgiving head –
this one here –
that still thinks it can rearrange the days
like playing cards – re-shuffle the dead.
This head that let you down –
long before and far too much –
abandoning your wedding to the commotion of my fears.
Or in earlier days – an urchin child,
cast beneath your teenage status of condescending.
And not possessing the glowing emblem
of your grammar school cap,
I wore it in private, but with a similar authority,
while you were out with the burden of ambitious friends,
combing your hair like a Kennedy.
We all played our role on Sellars Road,
and no part was greater than any other.
We were the perfect choice of an unseen god
and a loving mother.
And you did not deserve to die,
tethered to a bed of tubes and ignorance.
I wanted to lift you up and drive you to the coast –
wrapped in a swaddling cloth – or just a coat.
To release you there, like a free balloon,
to die in the dignity of arcadian air.

Inside a loyal, but immature clock –
the one that ticked around my wooden youth,
in those restless days, with little to do,
except unfold the idealist hours.
I was lost inside that strict young box –
clicking its seconds towards an imaginary hour;
a cornered soul, in love with rhythms,
and hoping your body might move with mine.
I ticked along with deafening chimes
that reverberated into my veins, like vines,
and caught my clothes in relentless cogs;
of this awkwardly spinning, clockwork box –
this beating heart that gave no clue
of what time the outside hands might say –

III. Zeus Inside My Clock

or in a timely way, would have impatience do.
I was rarely older than the previous day
and never older than this clock of glue –
this daily clock, which was starting to give way –
to polished resentment of who we are.
I eventually emerged with time to spare –
and with countless adolescent hours of despair.
Until I realised what would be best for me
was well beyond this imaginary stare.
Inside a loyal, but immature clock –
the one that ticked around my wooden youth,
in those restless days, with little to do,
except unfold the idealist hours.
I was lost inside that strict young box –
clicking its seconds towards an imaginary hour;
a cornered soul, in love with rhythms,
and hoping your body might move with mine.
I ticked along with deafening chimes

Zeus Inside My Clock

Inside a loyal, but immature clock –
the one that ticked around my wooden youth,
in those restless days, with little to do,
except unfold the idealist hours.
I was lost inside that strickening box –
clicking its seconds towards an imaginary hour;
a cornered soul, in love with rhythms,
and hoping your body might move with mine.
I swung along with deafening chimes
that reverberated into my veins, like vines,
and caught my thoughts in relentless cogs,
in this awkwardly spinning, clockwork box –
this beating heart that gave no clue
of what time the killer hands might say –
or in a timely way, would have impatience do.

I was rarely older than the time of day
and never older than this clock of glue –
this daily clock, which was starting to give way –
a polished resentment of who we are.

I eventually emerged with time to spare –
and with countless adolescent hours of despair.
I realised then, what would be best for me,
was beyond the semaphore-hands of now –
or the full face of time – with that numeric stare.

Her Twinset Face

At the announcement of supposed good news
her face never changed:
Good news always comes with bad – it is the way –
that's what she'd say:

"Good news and bad are a pair –
a twinset of pain and strawberry hair."

Who could not see the balance of that?
A quiet jumper, shrouded with a shroud.
A cardigan that smiled out-loud –
both perfectly in and out of fashion at the same time.
It was a diametric, weighing on joy
like a knitted cloud.

God knows how she got out of bed, but she did.

Her face would never change though –
a neutral face, of neither embarrassment nor shame –
always hinting possibilities of mistaken blame:

"It was merely the product of life's heartbreaking bile,"
(her body smiling its bodily smile).

God knows how she said hello, but she did.

A Human Crisis

An old woman –
sitting in a living room
amongst a family of portraits
in a disintegrating world.
Not caring to eat.
Not daring to care.
Too frightened to go out
into that...
unfamiliar air.
Unsure what had greyed
her colourful life –
the voices of children –
the husband; the wife?

She photographs herself with a mobile phone
just to confirm she is alone.

There are ghosts in the air
and there is also despair.
Where life collided –
into a favourite chair.

Written on a Wall in London

A lament to Blur – with a notion of hope.

When you said that modern life is rubbish,
having seen it as graffiti in Bayswater Road,
life was not as bad as the future gets –
there was Blur and Oasis then – alcohol and cigarettes.
The Kinks and the Beatles were almost gone –
except in the voice of new and echoed song.
Sometimes when I think back
I can hear Eleanor Rigby coming on.

So if 'Modern life is rubbish'
was written on every toilet wall
of all the gin joints in all the towns in all the world,
why is she still leaving home?

Fate Gets off at the Next Stop

He was knocked down by a London bus
while crossing Abbey Road at ten-fifty-one –
or was it ten-fifty-two? I cannot swear;
I was distracted by the length of his gorgeous hair...
(and the label stuck to the sole of his shoe).
It does not matter which minute stopped his breath,
life is not measured in buses or clocks,
only by death.

The bus was on schedule – but so was his day –
and there is no available embrace to weep;
no more timely a street for death to lay.
And no particular shoulder for the purpose of blame.
It was a shame... that is all we can say.

Sorry You Are Late

Sorry I am late – I left the house on time
but I deliberate – inventing new words
that mean the same as death,
but not so harsh, or so left to trust.
Not so washed in forlorn consonants
and the latent tears of uneasy vowels.
I am never comfortable attending funerals –
especially those of my dearest words.
So here are eulogies – impossible to say,
that I revoke my power, even to pronounce.

And now it is your turn to be dead
I must apologise for being late myself.
I certainly did not wish to offend –
it is just that my heart – in this broken state
found it difficult to attend.

A Moment is Always Too Late

O Golden throne. Golden throne.
Sit you down in the corner of my gloom.
Let me die in the curving shape of remembered arms –
a soft, warm interlude of glorious embrace.
Let me sing of oblivion with a mask on my face –
and with the essential ruins
falling about my feet.

No God Decreed the World to be Negatively Polite

Sometimes, there is a great deal of truth
in appalling comments.
And the future of our civilisation
depends upon the admission
of inhibiting facts.
No god decreed the world should be barren of thought,
or ignorant of all strands of suffocating dogma.
Or negligent of the illusions of social equality.
Or to part with its dignity, to suffer an enemy.
And no god decreed our culture be abandoned
just to instil an unbalanced sense of virtue –
that poison in the well of socialised evil,
currently seething in a vicious woke.

Word Zero

Who are we to suggest
what time has in store for the iron in our souls?
It is our burden to live our lives
in misery, happiness, glory or understatement –

not necessarily trust.

I choose understatement.
It may contain all of the above –
including rust.

The Old Skills of Applied Austerity

We live our lives like fugitives in the rough and tumble –
a chanting of souls who fear no evil.
As bathers, without soap or water.

When we are all strewn across the post-apocalyptic chaos,
we, the eternal peasants, will be a revelation to behold.
Accustomed to pain and the simple devotions,
we will teach you all –
you surprised and manicured people.
We will teach you the skills you will need for coping
in the face of a sudden and universal malevolence –
in the jaws of an abyss you refused to revoke.

We live our lives like fugitives in the rough and tumble –
stand aside and we will guide you home.

2017

City Limits

Hate the word exurb.
It takes me out of myself.
Prefer the gutter.

Haiku 5/7/5 syllables

First published on Twitter – 13th March 2022

The Microphone of Love

The microphone of love
is a terrible thing.
It whispers all our comments
into the smothering street.
Where the burden of semantics
deranges all our words
and our hearts are ever swollen
by this bullying betrayal.

I saw you at the bus stop
heading for a plane
to fly you out to anywhere
and lose me in the game

Love's microphone was listening
but you never said a word.
You went away, not in silence,
but singing like a bird.

The Anomaly of Human Existence

This is a crow – with a raised beak,
carefully placed between its presence
            and your eye.
It marks your limits with this dangerous stick,
and with a precise suspicion –
thinking only of its place.
This is the centre of the scene,
which is the centre of the world –
having not much distance.
The fading fields and rampart hills
are of no consequence and are made of mist;
which in any case, is all there is
of this cosmos of crow – this place –
            this corvid space
you wandered into by mistake.

Animals know mankind is different –
and because of our peripherals
we are something fake.
The crow keeps a distance of maintained good sense –
its cage of feathers, hiding hearts of lizards –
or wrens or cats or cows or snakes –
and there is no space between the crow's existence
and the avoidance of death –
that daunting enquiry – in each animal face.

Autumn in Iowa

For my friend Catherine Tudor

I had to write in autumn – your favourite season.
I think of you prodding the smoking leaves
and wondering about Halloween –
what you can do to surprise your cats;
something not yet seen.

They have already spied their own eyes,
reflected in glass as evening darkens.
And they are suspicious now of everything –
even of themselves – it is that time of year.

And they have witnessed the auburn falls,
that you relinquished to this pumpkin hour –
and the vampire lour you love so much,
with its innocuous glance toward trick or treat.
They have heard the doorbell ring, soft and sweet –
and your dancing through the house
with the hell of sweets.

And you will always have the comfort of song
as the nights settle down to far too long.

Your heart – the heart I know,
is lit by the colour of translucent skins –
those leaves that hang like copper shields

on the glowing veins of idle trees.
They guard all joy against this failing air,
now stripped bare to a cooler breeze.
Yet wrapping the sky in Sunday silk –
slick and light as Fred Astaire,
to dance a last waltz in the spinning force
of a spent tornado's expiring breath.

You have waved goodbye, with a fanning hand,
to the oppressive heat of summer nights
that fall now comes to cool away –
coalescing the sunset into a thinner light –
and with sunburned shadows,
strung with lace and ghostly tight –
they bind the whole of Iowa
and all the Midwestern states,
as they merge into the shared gold
of a faithful honey.

The Way to Roethke

To the memory of Theodore Roethke. 1908-1963

Does anyone know the way from here?
To nowhere in particular – just from here.
Places tire us awfully well
and even though we are not inspired
by the magnet pull of anywhere else,
there will inevitably be a need to go –
the shallow walls of boring rooms
have decreed it so.
I may try the far fields of Roethke,
with their agreeable tones that run like milk.
He had a singing about his gentle voice
that shone through words, like temperate fire,
illuminating every subtle desire,
to pass them on, in all transparency.
He was a projector with a rolling film,
focussing the rhythm of his ploughing wake.
He hung fresh words, floating on the air –
wafting in the wind of a washing line,
where even now they breathe again,
clean and true, if not quite dry.
So does anyone know the way from here?
At least to the far fields, if not beyond –
to the eccentric heart of a borrowed man,
of these – and still more darker times,
who promised our eyes would begin to see.

4

What is living about? I do not know.
It may have something to do with you and me,
but I am sure there was never anything specific said –
no future to be discovered or disclosed?
Nothing beyond this breathing body,
from where we now try to look ahead and see.
It doesn't matter that we are human, or a tree.
Not in a fleeting inhalation of tantalising smoke,
none of us could blow free or catch –
for fear of burning our fingers
on an expiring cigarette or flaring match.
Anything that marks time is as cruel as a clock –
even a door – and the dropping of a latch.
There was some talk of religious proof

IV. The Silent Hill

but it was just an after-death response,
designed to allay our steepest fears
and prove that what is true – is already ours.
A foil to freedom – a price on our heads –
a sentence – to be paid in millions of years.
There is no truth either, in the silent stones,
regardless of how carefully they are planted on the hill.
Or how many days of flowers and tears
we will to and fro – adding to the bill.
What is living about? I do not know.
It may have something to do with you and me,
but I am sure there was never anything specific said –
no future to be discovered or disclosed?
Nothing beyond this breathing body,
from where we now try to look ahead and see.
It doesn't matter that we are human, or a tree.
Not in a fleeting inhalation of tantalising smoke,

Flashlight & Valkyrie Coming In
To Judith

On this frost-laden night
when the washing hangs solid
and frozen white –
cut out of cold and eerily stiff –
hanging like death on the icicled line.
My mother goes out in chosen boots
to pick up the dead of a winter battle.
She is carrying a basket of hunted shadows;
each victim corresponding
to their redeemable pain.

Father at the doorway with a searching light –
his precious torch, scouring bitter air.
It sparkles diamonds on frosted sleeves
and skirts and socks that will not bend.
These are the rigid, frozen beings
that haunt our clothes with winter strife.
They live in the steam of our exhaled breath,
absorbing death – to resuscitate their form.

The door is soon closed onto this bitter night,
that would stiffen we children, same as these clothes.
It would harden our skin with an infinite death,
to glisten like garments in a searching light.

Lincoln Cathedral Love Song

For Catherine Sales

"Flower in the crannied wall,
I pluck you out of the crannies,
I hold you here, root and all, in my hand,
little flower."

   Alfred Lord Tennyson. 1808-1892

When I saw you again after thirty-eight years,
our waving smiles
collided into moments –
those ancient and unfinished minutes
a cathedral's walls can hold in perpetuity.

We cannot deny love, even though it may detach
in the long distance of circular time.
For love can also hang-fire too –
even on decisions made without regress.
It hides in the cracks of antique stone;
or in the heavenly glass of lancet or rose;
till we come looking again – for familiar love –
or just our past in perfect repose.

We are inquiring partners – better than friends,
armed with a history of losses and dead ends.
And there will be no leaf or stone unturned
in this sudden search for lost selves.

Even though we are easily found –
lightly buried beneath
unnecessary charade –

that of coy looks and timid hugs,
and a noble resistance to
impish doubt.

And once rediscovered – or found out –
lost love wants for nothing,
like a once orphaned child.

We have always known exactly
where we left our hearts –
in those unforgotten miles
of crannied walls –
of waves and smiles.

From Beauty Has Grown Ambition

Your kite attacked my head – on purpose.
And having looked into its murderous face
and studied the extremes of a lethal expression,
I can see it acted purely on the instincts
of a soulless, loyal possession.

But the beast is uncontrollable now;
certainly for one so tender as you –
expecting a deft touch to work with everything –
even in a field, wearing a high-heeled shoe.

Not to mention a lack of concentration
and a reliance on the tenuous nature of glue.

You no doubt glanced from your duty of care –
wondering why my embarrassment had a guilty stare;
a pink balloon, amid the verdant bracken –
you may even have detected a distant obsession.
The kite then homed-in on your neglected focus
and attacked my head with frightening aggression.

Did you not feel the kite line slacken?

I suppose you thought I was the stalking kind –
standing and staring from the edge of the woods?
And I honestly admit that may be true,

because I certainly feel delinquent now –
with my brain-damaged head
needing the therapy of glue.

It is clearly not my fault though –
this whole dilemma revolves around you.
Your beauty has captured
my obsessive ambition
and controls my yearnings with a string.

Spoken Through Helium

Liberals want everyone to speak like them.
Yet they have nothing to offer
but the fear of their values.
Even holy men may squirm at this concocted legislation
and its obsessive calls for the intervention of virtue.
It will soon become the burden of a hateful reign;
to have us all jostling on their cherished edge:
that naïve latitude of impractical equality
that can no longer hold its peace in marriage.

Which part of our freedoms will these cowards seek out,
to condemn, persecute and casually detain?
Where else will this treacherous storm of spite
unload its grievous ressentiment of distain?

On the hustings, they breathe in helium balloons;
providing the aspect of lunatic voices –
wanting everyone to chant the ignorance of crowds –
there are no other choices.

I Think That's What She Said?

Whose afraid of Virginia Woolf?

"The charm of London is that it is not built to last,
it is built to collapse..."

just after the usurping oligarchs
and the greed of land-grabbers
and the tax-haven millionaires
have all arrived on their golden bedsteads –
squeezing their way around idealist agendas,
yet comfortable with the old song of coming terror.
Their deepest pockets are filled with bullets,
and the ability to kill a wilderness of poets.
They use communist words that speak of money –
which is always the hallmark of rich propaganda.
The wrong sort of people appropriate the arts;
those we call cuckoos – who forge in the fire –
who replace the monuments of the compliant and gullible,
and build hollow trees from the eggs of birds.

(I think that's what she said?)

2017

The House of Democracy

You will not get my vote
and I will keep my truth –
after fifty years of lies, greed
and political folly,
your efforts at governance
have toppled my roof.

...And Having Writ – the Delusion Moves On...

There is no neat class system in Britain anymore –
it has been reconstructed in a greater chaos.
There is an underclass beneath the working class floor;
a caste system now – and so much more.
There are religious sects, divided by a common god,
and all the tribal nationalities
that intensify division.

But there is no simple class system in Britain anymore –
just the illusion of parity – and racism for sure.

*The worst thing about racism, apart from the obvious, is that both
Liberals and Fascists use it to build their high ground. Thus it becomes
the call of diversity in the guise of a bandwagons and on to the further
disruption of balance.*

Mistaken Identity

I once tripped over George Best –
he fell over in front of me
and I fell over him –
two clowns on the same page –
both motivated
by a search for abandoned things.
We helped each other stand
and brushed each other's civilian suits,
and on making our apologies –
saying our goodbyes,
we mistakenly walked into each other's lives.
I have been an outrageously good-looking
football legend ever since.
And George has immortalised himself
in the sobriety of words.

Youth is Either Wasted or Unsung

"Youth is wasted on the young" – George Bernard Shaw

The young think they are superheroes –
see them queueing for the challenge of theme parks;
squaring up to the next terrifying ride.
Or laying in a gutter on Friday nights,
singing abide with me... abide.

They have become ninja in their fuelled heads;
warriors that run amok for charitable events;
echoing the plight of abstract victims –
helping them say the unsayable
by dying in the foreground.

Youth is either wasted or unsung –
as they strive to live within a moral pledge.
But why should they listen to anyone old
when the world turned out the way it did?
Their schedule is easy to follow though –
and somewhat resembling my very own:

sex; party; sex; party; sex; sex; shopping;
travel; green issues; party; sex...

Unlike me, they will find their way home.

The Hobbit Trilogy of Films

The judgement of unfavourable reviews
is made lucid by the interpretations of false antiquity;
thinking northern dialects are sufficient
to translate the dark ages into devious deeds;
and some effects are enough to carry the brute energy
required to impart evil into the bones of men.
And all within a fantasy of sentimental reason,
and with the footloose paradigm of an unfixed age.
Some genuine witchery would be fitting here;
a whisper – scattered amongst leaves and fire.
It may even, in a neophyte sense,
be called true magic – or 'autumn's desire'.

Yet both would ring true,
including, as they do,
the songs of fruit and fire.

The mystique of the Hobbit depends on a lantern's magic,
where light and speed merge in vertical slits.
Some say they are magnificently contrived effects –
though it is hard to match the stealth
of unconscripted rainbows,
or the majestical portent of an actual eclipse.

Thus illusions bleed from the overripe colossus,
becoming tv advertising and its parody of tricks.

Yet far beneath the skill of true magical eloquence,
such as the ancient guidance of cast yarrow sticks.

The lantern lights the path to many riches,
as described in the piles of guarded gold.
These breathe in sleep, under a dragon's claws,
along with the necessary philosophers' stone.
All rest well, until disturbed by greed –
fevered adventurers, drenching ruthless hands;
feeling the drippings of golden desire,
running beneath the cracked mountain of Erebor.

Yet all should ring true,
including, as they do,
the fruit of fantasy and fire.

All aboard then – jump to this map!
Jump to this map of Middle Earth.
To the glistening southwest, on the edge of Gondor,
resplendent in the waters of the Bay of Belfalas –
There I spy Hollywood – in a golden ship –
sailing homeward to a glittering palace.

All Too Human

I live amongst machines now –
who do and say the right thing.
And even when they sing
it is only the song of an orderly choir.
They hum the salvation of approved desire
and are themed with the blasphemy
of a god's broken song.

These are the vaguest of the vague –
who dare not face their timely conclusions.
They fear a doubt will sound unforgiving;
too left or too right-wing.
Requested clarifications are smothered in denial,
until there is nothing – not a thing.

And it is never too late to turn away;
it is never a complex or difficult task
to herd the migraine out of the light –
that blinding wheel of denied science –
that indeterminable muse of postmodernist tease
that dismantles the zeitgeist
down to its knees.

"...that joke you were telling, a while ago...
about deconstructing the idea of proof –
will laughter be acceptable in the coming year?

Will it be criminal to defend an uncomfortable truth?
There are ruthlessly imposed strictures here;
enforced by the inherent hammer of the weak –
or by that sword of Damocles above every head –
now silenced – afraid to speak."

Do not discard your right to inquiry –
to err is human – to seek freedom is divine.
Do not be persuaded you are ill with phobias –
trust yourself and your covenant of thoughts.

The rightful plans for human survival
all come with a sudden and frightening chill.

There is No Sign to Armageddon

There is no arrow towards Armageddon,
just a slow lurching of the ocean tides.
The carbon swords have already splinted
and there is only the murk of lucrative industry.
There is no signpost to the final battle;
humankind instinctively knows the way.
And feeling at the pocketed paper invitation,
we are confident in the hope of a welcome ovation.
Yet humankind's default state is misery and pity:
the battle – the war – is just a commotion.
A chance to serve in the loudest army.
Each missile ends with a deluge of angels.

The Truth of Distractions

In the game of '*humans create and humans destroy*',
there is no sadder part than 'humans destroy'.
Their carefree guise – pathetic in their trust –
feels at one with an ignoble entropy.
It is proclaimed as the distraction of belated teamwork,
leaving gullible souls to obey devious rules.

Yet people will gradually learn to forget –
and eventually lean towards a fearful state.
One that arms the strong with careless weapons
and the weak with fate.

A Black Hole for Truth

i

The black hole of truth is never full –
there is always gravity for so much more.
Truth is poured in everyday,
from every continent and every shore;
from every blatant mind and lip;
from every pointing fingertip.
Its sides are as busy as Niagara falls,
consuming a dark pledge of hypnotic flood.
A deluge of thoughts in cascading waves
have abandoned hope to its deepest prayers –
a vacuous malaise.

We are all in make-up now;
all touched-up by current trends.
And by social media –
that inspired vacuum that never ends.
  *"It is a place where you are redefined
  in a polite smudge of abundant friends."*

O Twitter, Twitter on the wall,
who has the fairest followers of all?
  *"Twitter, Twitter – the world needs a babysitter –
  the world needs a little more Instagram glitter."*

ii

Who is this face you dispense like a whore –
and why don't I see my own avatar anymore?
   "It is not a face that you would recognise
   amongst thousands more."

iii

I am sure there is truth in the warmth of the soul.
Yet what darkness prevails behind the orbits of the eyes?
They look baffled – and wear a hint of surprise,
aware of the god-cave in the dome of the skull?
   "They will need to expand into a shrinking abyss –
   the collapsing folds of an agent mind.
   And woman or man, they shall all feel the peace,
   of a fading obscurity that weak energy will bind."

Is it time for another tweet already?
Some trick to prise our fingers off the ledge?
To mask the promise of an unheard truth
and let it slip beyond the edge?

2016

The Silent Hill

What is living about? I do not know.
It may have some business with you and me?
But I am sure there was never anything specific said –
no future to be discovered or disclosed?
Nothing beyond these breathing souls –
that try to look ahead and see.
It does not matter that we are forests of humans,
or a single tree.

Not in a tantalising inhalation of smoke
that must blow wild; and none may catch.
For fear of burning awkward thoughts
on an expiring cigarette or a flaring match.
That which marks time is as cruel as a clock –
even a door – and the dropping of a latch.

There was some talk of religious proof,
but it was just the aftermath of an agreed response –
designed to allay our steepest fears
and prove that what is really true – is only ours;
a foil to freedom – with a price on our heads –
a sentence – to be paid in millions of years.
And there is no truth either – in the silent stones,
regardless of how carefully they are planted on the hill.
Or how many days of flowers and tears
we will to and fro – adding to the bill.

Poems are never finished,
so you cannot rely on this one either.
I may return in a very few minutes,
or it may be an hour – who can tell?
In truth, I may never return at all –
I may not even be alive...
though that does not make this poem complete;
I may still have enough credit with God
to make one final tweak?
Just to be sure, keep an eye on my words,
they may start to reposition their form on the page –
or maybe call again next week?
↲ Poems are never finished,
so you cannot rely on this one either

5

V. Unfinished Thinking

I may return in a very few minutes,
or it may be an hour – who can tell?
In truth, I may never return at all –
I may not even be alive...
though that does not make this poem complete;
I may still have enough credit with God
to make one final tweak?
Just to be sure, keep an eye on my words,
they may start to reposition their form on the page –
or maybe call again next week?
There's a party to celebrate their coming of age, here's a
Poems are never finished,
so you cannot rely on this one either.
I may return in a very few minutes,
or it may be an hour – who can tell?
In truth, I may never return at all –
I may not even be alive...
to make one final tweak?

Stranger Still in Utility Sunlight

To the memory of Leonard Cohen. 1934-2016

Leonard, it is time for the Moon.
I know you are a poor lover of its simple ways
and think it somehow shallow,
but I still have a job to do;
a challenge to bear – and by the way,
I still think you retired too soon…

Okay then, Leonard, let us forget the Moon –
it is time for the Sun – the immersive Sun.
I think you entrusted your safety to the Sun
and that is why you left for noble Greece.
In fact, I think you are still there – writing:
perhaps a third novel –
'The Book of Longing for Something Else?'

The Sun is gracious – it minds its own business.
It shines our shoes – it keeps its distance.
It wears no mask or stranger's face.
It is a friend to our eyes in what it does best –
out there beyond our current position –
that of basking in the dividend
of legitimate shade.

First published in Fevers of the Mind Poetry *2021*

I Did Not Want It Darker

On the death of Leonard Cohen. 2016

When your song first idled in my head,
like something matured in careful words.
I was a student in my teens – exiled – un-said,
with no road for my drowning voice.

Your songs sang out of the influence of poems,
like a threading railway, forged in ruin –
rolling out your passion in Spanish chords
and the black brute of honest dread.

Lorca found his voice stifled by blood –
he, the designated hero of your noble campaign.
It was a blend of the stations of devotion and reason,
and all that lingers in songs and rooms.

You threw your baggage out onto the pavement –
into the anonymity of my least-walked streets.
And that day I saw a founding step –
a revolution, intertwining words and thoughts.

You sang above the abandon of amorous poets,
who closed their lips and proceeded to go blind.
While you, with your Kestrel eye,
ranged the glories they vowed to overlook.

The implicit technicalities of love and being
were flicked away and left behind,
as they talked themselves naked, with the spoken word,
immersed in the self-sabotage of liberty's dissent.

You elevated your poems on the wings of chords,
so a wider audience might comprehend
not only the unfathomed void of a broken heart
but the subtle things you had to sing to mend.

And they were each caught then, by the siren voice,
as all we disheartened sailors were.
And all soon fevered with a charming blend
of patience, love and rapturous doom.

It was the poems though, that spoke to my longing,
from the grey cities of smoke and gold –
out of an avalanche of hidden critics
who discussed your darkness in curtained rooms.

And with an inability to hear without eyes,
they made their own dark song to sing.
It rang in the certainty of eventual prose,
walking through pages of worn-out words.

I Did Not Want It Darker – continues

In time, eased by the celibacy of your charm,
they smoothed themselves with forgiveness and love.
They found a shoe that fit better as a glove –
thus perceiving the so-called 'Godfather of Gloom'.

It was a dagger through your triumphant heart –
a tenderly savage paper dart –
but washed off – like the crayons they used
to eventually scribble a favourable report.

Your poetry spoke into the mind and the heart –
and always with music, as it lent itself to you.
Always with a resonating chord or two,
strummed by a lost soul, reaching out.

If only for those troubling minor chords
that leave the soul vibrating on
with increased emotion and subdued doubt –
an attempt to set a few words free –

an attempt to capture truth, and smooth it out.
To push the sky beyond a pilgrim's thoughts.
To stop the clock and make it wait –
                to instigate – to celebrate –
those same words in perhaps a less apparent state.

Words we would never really need to own,
or reveal the joke inside their frown.
Or think of as correct, or right –
but simply called upon in the delicate night.

Such words once said, need never be recalled,
they move their meaning, where other's take flight.
For they have already snapped their core – like flares –
and bathed us in a blesséd light.

First published in Fevers of the Mind Poetry – October 2021

This is Silence

On the death of Leonard Cohen. 2016

Thank you for filling the silence
with a wisdom we could claim.
Thank you for filling the darkness
with a holy flame.

You sat at your usual table;
we gathered your final light –
as you spread your words like playing cards
and signed a treaty with the night.

We followed the lines of your poems,
and your songs, with their luminous thought,
that now become rumours of our own demise –
in this field of wounded hearts.

So until then, and though we have your song,
we will miss your breath of carefulness
in a silence that seems wrong.

First published in Fevers of the Mind Poetry – October 2021

Unfinished Thinking

Poems are never finished,
so you cannot rely on this one either.
I may return in a very few minutes,
or it may be an hour – maybe later?

In truth, I might never return –
I may not even be alive to do so...
though that does not make this poem complete –
I may have God's forgiveness for a final tweak?

Just to be sure, keep an eye on my words;
they may reposition their form on the page.
Or why not call again next week?
There's a party to celebrate their coming of age.

A Day on Claypit Lane

To Kathleen: my brother's wife and a fan of Dylan. 1967.

Listening to Dylan – a Saturday invitation –
to view the new house,
in its system of shared ages.
What memories draw me back there –
to that valued day of welcome.
Where beginnings were accepted
in a saga of emergence.
There is a baby sleeping and a feeling of well-being.
He dreams the songs of Dylan in sheets of falling words.
Kathleen hosts proceedings
with an effortless perfection; a welcome – like salvation;
a journey worth the way.

The new house shared a hillside
with many different levels.
So I took a turn at digging
at some needed excavation.
We were straightening the landscape
where the water lost its bearings;
where we hung it out like bedsheets
and set the air to drying.

It was a bond of something broader –
a span of wide ambition.
A volume shy of Camelot, but without the cost of illusion.
A theory of redemption – with its stray ideas of freedom,

that broke the chains of seeing
beyond the ruins of Northern blues.

There were dreams of empire waiting
in my far investigations;
of the places I was going – in my free-wheeling way.
I was never keen on Dylan, but admired his new orations.
His words all faced the future
in their streams of holy power.

We also played the Beatles (in the voice of Billy Shears)
with the help of spinning records
at the centre of our being.
Yet I knew too many minutes
would cause my mind to waiver.
So I bid a restless farewell
with a travelling student's valour.

We were safe in that young vortex
of lyrical understanding.
I would like to be there now,
had the world not missed a turning.

A Lack of Effort in Wider Thought

The world is waiting for broader thought;
its philosophical endeavours now arrive with pictures.
They no longer map the values of intricate ideas –
those paths we might take – or stretch time to chart.
Everything becomes *now* – with the given luxury of fake.

Only trite adventures in *photomentology*
(an enhanced discolouration of human sight)
seem to offer an Earth's-worth of human transcending;
or search beyond the beauty of saturated denial .
They bleed into the canvas of falsified empathy –
of politics, therapy and stylised pity.
They have become so limited in their possessive scope
we will barely need a moment to review their praise.

Thought has descended into ideology and fables –
and the love-soaked lines that beg us to cry.
What it means to say, bears little scrutiny
beyond a shallow ear or the marbled eye.
That frozen stare of colossal beauty
that fails its substance and has no words.
It ceases to draw us any further inward –
towards the enormous singularity
of the cosmological heart.

Missed Kiss

Even after thirty years of kissing
our lips still miss in the dark.

Discarded Genius

When genius falls into the room
do not be looking the other way –
at some meagre triumph of word-play
that sits on the page like a card trick –
one that delights all reason, then makes you sick –
that shatters no windows – even tied to a brick.
When genius limps into the gorgeous room,
grovelling high, on its wasted knees,
its energy may be too bright for your lamp
or may miss its own moment –
turning up like a tramp.
It may be too subtle and catch in your hair
or carve faint clues in the back of a chair.
It may be waved into oblivion by a modest smile,
or be swept away by mile on mile
of eager words that deafen all ears
and damage the air for a hundred years.
We all have our moment – our flag to unfurl –
yet art is an avalanche – it can smother the pearl.

A Hex on the Anointed

I came down from the mountains
to listen to the people.
They hated each other
and spoke with dark malice.
They had grown their own cancer
with a murderous media
who dealt in histrionics
and preordained conclusions.
There was no rationality,
only febrile monstrosity,
while the West bewitched its heart
with a mistaken woke...
and with the accepted guilt;
and the rotten heartache;
and the terrible self-doubt
of a wounded conscience.

They did envy the mountains though –
those static lords –
keeping as always, a perfect distance.
I will return with a vision –
wide and calling –
a broader interpretation,
and a new kind of peace.

I Am Wanted at the Pandemic

The human race deserves the flood;
sit in your gardens and die of water.
Or wait until the Sun explodes,
or something sooner.
Something more refined,
that does not involve laughter;
that has no cure or shape or shelter.
Something a scientist will be proud of
later.

Understanding Chaos

There is nothing here but the fullness of summer,
with its birds and beaks
tapping out the hollow sound of hours.
Of many hours; of many moments;
of many summers on reseeded ground.
There is nothing here but the whole of summer.
I will make my sacrifice to imagined gods.

The Future

I am always disappointed by rumours of the future –
it never quite seems to arrive complete.
I have always been hopeful though,
and think I can see it – out there in the offing –
a grey ship in the blur.
It is no doubt full of enchanting cargo
that we push our will forward, just to imagine.
A puzzling shell, harbouring mysterious secrets –
and clues that promise everything –

and Hell.

Or perhaps it holds the metaphysical things –
should that be the way of future longing?
A voice that promises debatable triumph,
against hypocritical spirits chanting derision.
They shout down claims for empirical truth,
while accepting charmed prayers and golden apples.

But about the comedy of progress,
we shall not care –
it would be worth the journey
just to stare.

Dogma leads to the trends of hysteria:
like the mobile phones of social media;

ways to gossip about redundant things
or just words of hope that find no saviour.
All of which leaves us adrift in the offing,
with ever-suspicious and imprudent behaviour –
and the bedlam world we might create,
given another discarded and camouflaged clue.

A Firing Squad

Finding no song in the blush of silence.

I have been defeated and will die tomorrow;
hoisted by my own, reckless charade.
Bereft of union and social purpose,
like a house sparrow
when the last roof is destroyed –

though I will seek to remain employed.

I can do the job with my eyes permanently shut;
death has never been a barrier for me,
and between my life and mundane work
it was always in the background –
an impudent smirk – a black horse funeral –
scuffing at the dirt.

And there will be no point in leaving this stage of earth
with a full bag of energies digging at its grit:
I want to be distraught; I want to be wrung out;
I want to be the burned out shell of human existence
and human doubt. I want to go with the knowledge
that the last train has left the station
and is out there singing in the beautiful distance.

I will help the authorities prevent my handprints
from smearing blood on their white-washed walls.

Such signs would represent a signature of awakening –
a graphic resurrection of my dying fall.
It would seem a parody of both portent and glory –
an embittered voice rising from the bullet holes.

These dangerous symbols are louder than guns
and might signal the rise of an idealist cause.
A sudden revolution, dripping pointless blood –
instigated by the frustration of a misconstrued word.

I will instead recommend an assembly point
for the remaining trees to stand and blossom.
Perhaps to gather the remaining light
of a rarely glimpsed moment of cheerful sun.

Here perhaps – when this courtyard is done?

When it has spilt its example of dissenter's blood.
Soon after the march of the firing squad.
Each tree planted with a loyal companion –
the enduring battalion of a summer god.

The City of Palms

You must keep the virtues
and the low volume of your populous.
And not be degraded
by the discomfort of turmoil.
That deafening cacophony
of the broadening minority
who seek to pull down
the palms of your Jericho.

To Die like Keats

I will live like Keats among the nightingales,
with fresh air and longing – and bending boughs
that reflect their thoughts in the sleep of lakes –
hiding the depths with their silvered sheets.
I will linger on this promised shore,
where swallows hunt and buzzards soar
in the bowl of preoccupied pastel sky.
I am at peace, for once –
though were this scene within thine eye,
I would be better born in respect to life.

There will be a folly in this lush Elysium
in which to sit and ponder the painted hour.
Watching the bridge for signs of travel –
we are always sought for the study of our passing.
The waistband-bridge pinches the classical form
of an irrigated land, reduced to perspective.
Its far-off edge, where art stagnates,
folds into ripples at a pond-shaped dam.
Distance is always a subtle kind of wedge –
a place where life tightens its secret screws;
a far-off pasture for our narrow mortality –
that unforgiving barrier; that incomplete view.
A glimpse of the reckless is a slender future,
only afforded by our arrival in its time,
where the balloon of the moment expands around us,

and we are always central to its perfect heart.

We see everything with the same measure;
we sense the deep mystery of a firmament sky.
Where the souls of trees reach up to gather
their reasoned aesthetics from an exquisite blue.
They try to live in its peaceful face,
disturbing its soup with a breath of paint –
as reddening veins burst another sunset
into the static murmuration of blistered clouds.
The day soon turns into dewdrops and stars,
where comets fly – and even Mars –
yet there is no war afoot, or unnecessary cause,
for such illness of the collective mind.
Only in the overarching stillness that reigns
in the covenant of death and lethal words.
You can see their small strokes in bright vermillion,
like trailing fingers above the shimmering lake;
that sudden shiver where our friendship drowned
in the perfect moment for quenching pain.

And all around, in vibrant air, the frogs croak
their poison song – as sharp as crystal and cooler now...
yet blood-born – rare.
I feel that chill beneath their stare.

Stars poke my head from behind their diamonds
and I am reduced to 'scientist' – without provable truth.
For although there is no clue behind our statements,
nothing will remain unsaid.
Knowledge writes with an elemental quill;
it could kill us if it wanted and no doubt will.
But it never gives back the message – once said,
they adorn library shelves – now largely fiction –
comfortable in the germane aesthetics of loyal creed.

And although I do not care, I could join you in that pool;
there is always room for one more learnèd fool...
and on the saddest days, I long, or yearn
to live as ash in a Grecian urn.
For I am tired of modern illnesses and suicides –
and have the same weak chest as historic days.
I could catch consumption here,
with my wheezing breath.
I could attract cholera or the black death.
Classical ailments are closer to nature
than the cancers and dementia that plague us now.
Like good wine or bad, the classics have their year,
and the negative immersion of willing capability.
I will drink this cool air and see if my parts betray me.
I will drink to oblivion and see if my absent-minded *Lethe*
dares to slay me.

Brothers Beyond Reach

I cried for my brother
who died so long ago
he is almost forgotten.

He will not be forgotten.
He will not be forgotten.

For I will live in these words
to tell you a story.
I will tell you the story
of my living brother.
Who died so long ago
he is almost forgotten –
but will not be forgotten –
he lives in these words.

And will not be forgotten.

Lightning Source UK Ltd.
Milton Keynes UK
UKHW011827061022
410052UK00004B/109/J